I love Christmas. Here I am celebrating when I was 3.

Here I am with my grandfather, during a visit with him and my grand-mother when they lived in Africa.

This is me with my father when I was 9 months old.

This is me with my great grandmother.

Me and Maya on a walk with our mom in Madison, Wisconsin.

Here I am with my mother at 2 months old.

My friends and me at law school graduation.

When I was 10 months old, I visited Jamaica. This is me with my mother and my grandfather on my dad's side.

I was so excited to have a new baby sister. Here she is at 2 months old.

Me with Mrs. Shelton in her kitchen.

At my law school graduation with my first grade teacher, Mrs. Wilson, and my mom.

SUPERHEROES
Are Everywhere

KAMALA HARRIS

Illustrated by Mechal Renee Roe

PHILOMEL BOOKS

Faster than a rocket ship! Stronger than a tidal wave! Braver than a lion! Superheroes always make the world better, no matter what goes wrong.

Whenever there's trouble, superheroes show up just in time. When I was a kid, I was sure that superheroes were everywhere, blending in with regular people, ready to do good at a moment's notice.

I was determined to find them, so I started my superhero search right at home.

It didn't take too long to find one! I noticed my mom had a magic touch. Her hugs made me feel warm, safe, and even strong. She knew I loved good food, so she taught me her secret recipes, and we'd create huge, delicious meals together for our friends and family. I even cooked some of the dishes all by myself!

"See, Kamala," my mom would say. "You can do anything if you put your heart in it and try hard, anything in the world."

My mom was a superhero because she made me feel special. She believed in me, and that helped me believe I could do anything.

make you feel special.

Who makes you feel special?

Heroes are people

My sister, Maya, and I did everything together—ballet class, piano lessons, bike riding, and board games. I knew that if I ever needed her, she'd be there, one half of our dynamic duo.

When we felt sad, my mom would throw us an "un-birthday party" so we'd feel better. Together, we'd eat un-birthday cake, open un-birthday presents, and dance around the living room. Maya was always by my side.

My sister was a superhero because she was someone I could count on.

Who can you count on?

you can count on.

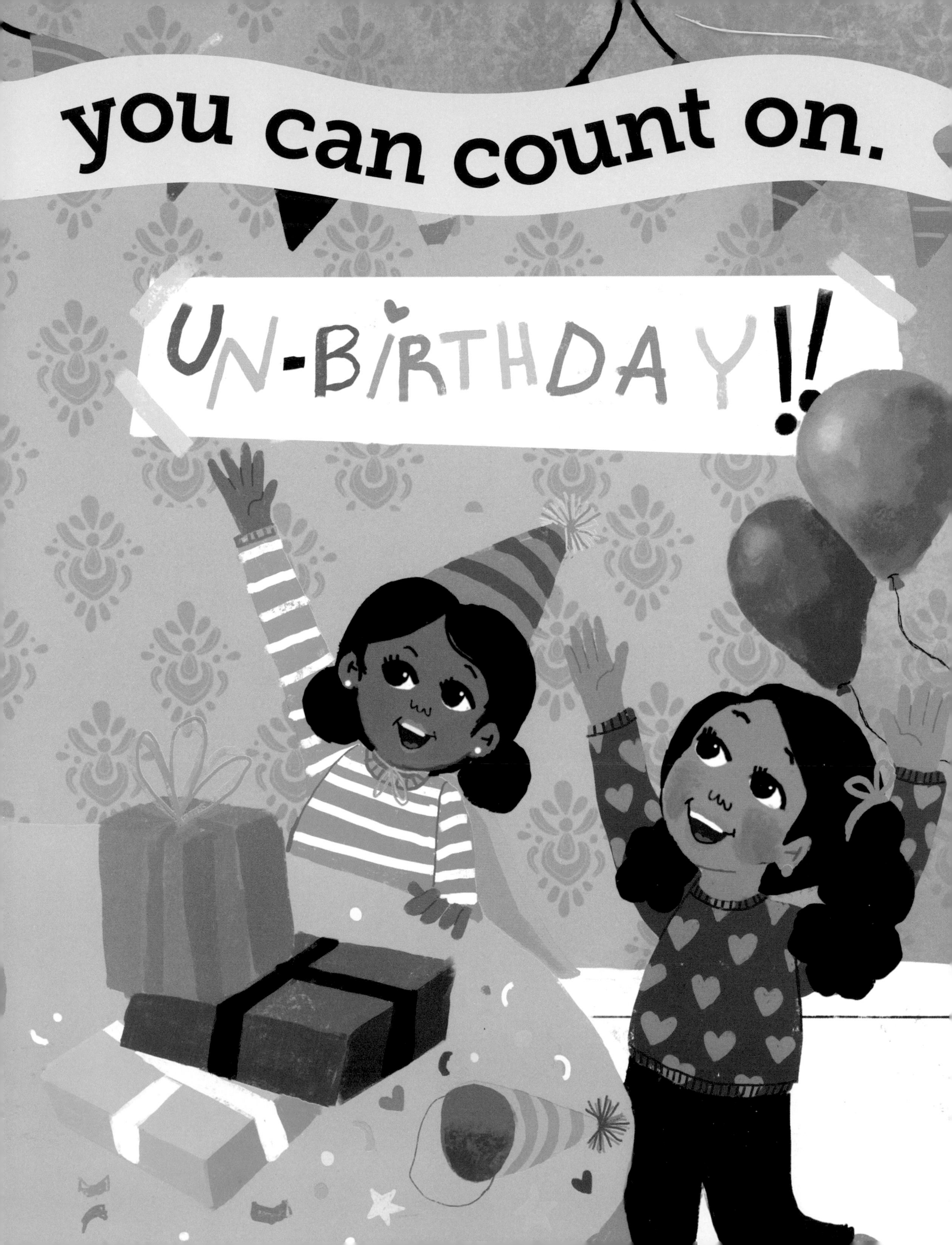

Heroes make you feel brave.

I kept searching for superheroes in other parts of my family.

My dad wanted me to be fearless. Whenever we were at the park, he'd let go of my hand and call out, "Run, Kamala, run!" and I'd run as far as I could for as long as I could.

My dad was a superhero because he made me feel brave.

Who makes you feel brave?

Heroes

My grandmother was one of the smartest people I've ever met. And she used her smarts and her voice to speak out for women who were being hurt and to teach them how to stay healthy.

stand up for what's right.

My grandfather used his voice to make India a free country.

All of my grandparents in India and in Jamaica were superheroes for standing up for what's right.

Who stands up for what's right in your life?

Heroes are

My best friends and I cared about each other. When I was in kindergarten I told a boy to stop teasing one of my best friends, and another time that best friend helped me when I fell on the playground. We all wanted to feel safe at school.

stand up for what's right.

My grandfather used his voice to make India a free country.

All of my grandparents in India and in Jamaica were superheroes for standing up for what's right.

Who stands up for what's right in your life?

Heroes are

My best friends and I cared about each other. When I was in kindergarten I told a boy to stop teasing one of my best friends, and another time that best friend helped me when I fell on the playground. We all wanted to feel safe at school.

best friends.

My best friends were superheroes because they made one another feel safe.

Who are your best friends?

Heroes are teachers.

I loved my first grade teacher, Mrs. Wilson. She taught us about plants and flowers, sang songs with us from cultures around the world, and revealed how tadpoles turned into frogs.

Teachers like Mrs. Wilson are superheroes because they show us the whole wide world and help us chase our dreams.

Who are your favorite teachers?

When I looked, I found a superhero right down my street!

Mrs. Shelton was our family friend and was like a second mom to me. She watched Maya and me while our mom was at work. We'd gobble up her homemade biscuits, peach cobbler, and gumbo for special occasions, and pile into her car on Sundays for church. Mrs. Shelton treated everyone with love and respect.

Heroes are kind.

Her kindness made her
a superhero to me.

Who is kind to you?

Heroes explore with you.

Aunt Lenore and I chased fireflies and caught them in jars. Uncle Sherman taught me to play chess. Aunt Mary and I read book after book together, and Uncle Freddy took me to museums where we'd see dazzling artwork.

My aunts and uncles—my mom's friends who were part of our family—helped me explore my world, and that made them superheroes.

Who helps you explore?

HOWARD University

Even as I got older, I kept searching for superheroes.

When it was time for me to go to college, I was excited to go where my aunt Chris went to study, at Howard University. My grandmother hadn't had the chance to go to college, but she encouraged her kids—my mom and my aunts and uncle—to study hard, and they did. My mom became a scientist, my uncle Balu is an economist, my aunt Sarala is a doctor, and my aunt Chinni works with computers.

They were superheroes because they showed me that by working hard, I could be whatever I wanted to be when I grew up.

Heroes work hard.

Who do you know who works hard?

After college, I wanted to become a lawyer like some of the people I looked up to—Thurgood Marshall, Constance Baker Motley, and Charles Hamilton Houston. They fought in court because they knew that people aren't always treated equally, but should be. Like them, I wanted to make sure that the law would protect everyone.

These lawyers were superheroes because they protected people by using the power of words and ideas.

Who protects you?

Heroes make a

difference, together.

Once I became a lawyer, and then a senator,
I worked with all sorts of people to help kids.
Even better, I got to know amazing kids who want
to make the world a better place.

And you know what I learned?

Heroes are . . . YOU!

Superheroes are everywhere you look! Even inside of you!

- Are you kind, brave, and curious?
- Are you a best friend?
- Do you share?
- Do you treat people fairly?
- Do you lend a hand when other people need help?

You're a hero by being the very best YOU.

Now that's pretty super!

The Hero Code

Do you want to be a superhero?

It's easier than you think.

The first thing to do is raise your right
hand and say the words on the next page out loud.
If you want to wear a cape while you do this,
you can—but you don't have to!

I PROMISE TO:

- ⭐ make people feel special
- ⭐ be someone people can count on
- ⭐ help people be brave
- ⭐ stand up for what's right
- ⭐ be a best friend
- ⭐ be a good teacher
- ⭐ be kind
- ⭐ explore with my friends and family
- ⭐ study and work hard
- ⭐ protect people who need it
- ⭐ make a difference when I can

I promise to be the very best me I can be!

A Timeline

October 20, 1964   I was born in Oakland, California.

January 30, 1967   My sister, Maya, was born.

1970   I started first grade in Mrs. Wilson's class.

1976   I organized a protest at my apartment building to let kids play in the yard, which had been off limits. We got permission to play there!

1984   I interned for Senator Alan Cranston of California and learned about what it was like to help make laws that make our country better.

1986   I graduated from Howard University with a degree in political science and economics.

1989   I graduated from the University of California's Hastings College of the Law.

1990   I officially became a lawyer and started working in the district attorney's office in Oakland. Every time I had to stand before a judge, I was proud to say, "Kamala Harris, for the people."

# of My Life

1998   I joined the San Francisco district attorney's office as the leader of the Career Criminal Unit.

2000   I joined the San Francisco city attorney's office, where I led a department that helped children and families.

2003   I ran for district attorney of San Francisco. My campaign slogan was "Kamala Harris, a Voice for Justice." I won the election with the help of hundreds of volunteers.

2010   I was elected attorney general of California. (I was the first woman and first person of color to have this job!)

2014   I married Douglas Emhoff. (He is also a lawyer!)

November 8, 2016   I was elected to the United States Senate as a senator from California. (I was the second African American woman and the first person of Indian descent to be elected to the Senate!)

January 3, 2017   I was sworn in to the 115th United States Congress.

To all the children in my life, and the most recent additions,
Amara and Leela. —KDH

To my mom, sisters, friends, and family,
and my high school teacher Ms. Shapiro. —MRR

PHILOMEL BOOKS
An imprint of Penguin Random House LLC, New York

Copyright © 2019 by Kamala Harris.
Art by Mechal Renee Roe. Photos courtesy of the author.
Penguin supports copyright. Copyright fuels creativity, encourages diverse
voices, promotes free speech, and creates a vibrant culture. Thank you for
buying an authorized edition of this book and for complying with copyright laws
by not reproducing, scanning, or distributing any part of it in any form without
permission. You are supporting writers and allowing Penguin to continue to
publish books for every reader.

Philomel Books is a registered trademark of Penguin Random House LLC.

Visit us online at penguinrandomhouse.com

Library of Congress Cataloging-in-Publication Data is available upon request.
Printed in the United States of America.
ISBN 9781984837493

10 9 8 7 6 5 4 3 2 1

Edited by Jill Santopolo.
Design by Jennifer Chung.
Text set in Mrs Eaves OT.
The art was done in Procreate.

My husband Doug and me at the ballpark.

Me and Flat Stanley in front of the state capitol.

Me in front of the Kamoji bus during my Senate race.

Me getting sworn in to my second term as the attorney general of California. Doug is holding the bible.

Doug and me voting at the elementary school around the corner from our house.

Election night in the U.S. Senate race.

Me and my mom at the Chinese New Year parade. She went to a lot of events with me.

I was honored to give a speech to students at Howard University.

This is my sixth birthday party with my best friends.

I am 7 years old here.
This was one of my favorite jackets.

Me and Maya near a lake
in Madison, Wisconsin.

Maya and I loved dancing—and still do.

I loved my stuffed horse when I was a baby.

Me at 2 with my newly born younger sister.